WHERE THEY MEET

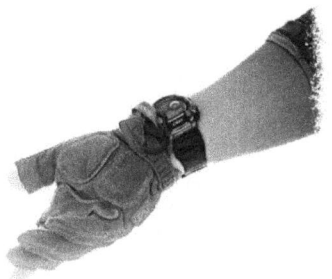

Where They Meet

Songs of War | Poems of Life

Cokie

Copyright © 2021 Cokie

All rights reserved.
This book or any portion thereof
May not be used or reproduced in any fashion whatsoever
Without the permission of the publisher or the author
Except for the use of quotations

Publisher: Dead Reckoning Collective
Book Cover Art & Design: Tyler James Carroll

Printed in the United States of America

ISBN-13: 978-1-7338099-8-6 (paperback)

To my wife, who is the reason I came back

To my children, who inspired so many of my words

To my parents and brother, who have read and suffered through everything I've written

To my brothers in the Marine Corps, National Guard, and the PMC world, who are the reason I keep going back

To my brothers specifically in the Shadow teams, who gave me a real war

To Claudio, whose name is etched in my flesh and soul

To Andy and Daniel, whose names are carried on in my blood

To those untouched by the following subjects, that you may know more

To my God, who gave me challenges and battles, the ability to succeed and (more frequently) fail, and ultimately my salvation through Christ

FOREWORD

Winston Churchill said that "history is written by the victors." But, where does that type of ruling leave a generation whose war hasn't ended? What can we say about the wars that go on for so long that a man can go fight, leave the military, return to the same theater as a civilian contractor, and then watch his child don the same uniform he did in his youth at the beginning of the conflict?

America's longest war will have many stories written of its victories and losses by the time it is over, whenever that day comes. But how will the victors be determined? Maybe it will be limited to those who "lived to tell the tale." Maybe it will be more than that. Maybe it will take more than survival. Maybe the true victors will be the ones who made it through and lived to make sense of it all and dared to put it on paper for others to learn from. To share the perspective of the ones who left boot prints in the dirt and blood on the uniform of the day.

In war, poetry has been an outlet for some and become a vocation for others for longer than anyone reading this has been alive. More importantly, it has been the habit of warriors to write and study it. Whatever portion of time and effort is dedicated to the pages, they will tell a story that deserves to be read and digested by the warrior class.

From the trenches of Somme to the tunnels of Cu Chi to the peaks of the Hindu Kush, the poet warriors of conflicts past and present will share this additional bond as warriors and wordsmiths. I have studied the work of poet warriors who came before us, and I believe that the words of Cokie will fall in line with his predecessors. His efforts will confirm that their words blazed a path for the generations to come. Students of history may remember my words, but they will remember his. His words will be studied as the names of those mentioned will be studied because they belong to the names etched in black granite. They belong to the names in reflective lettering on highway dedication signs. They belong to the names choked upon by the friends who lost them. They belong to the memories of quiet and cigarettes and trailer park philosophy that precede a gunfight.

Keith Walter Dow
Co-Founder of **Dead Reckoning Collective**

SONGS OF WAR

A Song of War	14
01 December 2005	15
A Prayer Before Mission	16
Warned Me	17
Mental Conditioning	17
Fatally Funneled	18
Shades	19
Hell-arious	20
Just Passing Through	21
Night Mission	22
Team Photo	23
The Newbie	24
The Old Hand	25
Old School	26
Civilization and Strife	27
FRAGO	28
Significant Mechanism of Injury	29
Dead Body	30
Purple Heart	32
The Stoned Old Man	34
From the Tower	35
Facets of Dying	36
Mainly Vice	36
Eating MRE's	36
God Bless Those Heathen Boys	37
Now is the Hour of Combat's Red Fire	38
The Over-Dramatic Private	39
Put Down Your Steel	40
A Song of Infantry	42
The Hide	44
Leftovers	45
Hypocrisy	46
Pity	46
What Were We	46
The Pure Warrior	47
Ask Me Now	48
The [Coward] Leader	50
The (Abridged) Afghan	51
Afghan Nights	52

POEMS OF LIFE

Song of Life	56
Autumn Indiana Drive	57
Finally Home	58
The Third Day	59
Hoosier Blonde	60
Let My Faith Be Bold and Wild	61
Metaphors	62

First World Problems 64
The Poet 65
Mongrels 66
My Forest 67
Her 68
My Son 69
Social Media 72
Old Deployment Bible 73
Plant a Garden, Young Warrior 74
Cowboy Dream 75
Peace or Comfort 76
Fire 77
Throw Me to the Fray 78
Compression 79
X 80
#49 81
Malachi 81
When is a Sunset Little More 82
Daughters 83
Weary Smile 84
What Beast is There Like Man 86

WHERE THEY MEET
Where They Meet 90
Warrior Faith 91
Truant Boy 92
Madly 93
Dream 93
Insomnia 94
Night Terrors 95
Dark Dreams 96
Parched 97
Lions 98
Transition Out 99
Sometimes No 100
2031 101
My Name is Veteran 102
Suicide 103
Cognitive Dissonance 103
Half Man (The Lament of LCPL Shmuckatelli) 104
Blurred Faces 106
Tell All My Girls 108
Absence 110
Prayers 111
Fallujah Man 112

Songs of War

A SONG OF WAR

To sing that Song of War
is the fate of the gunfighter.
Our nation espouses no god
mocks belief as quaint triviality.
Warriors thus forced make their own Molech
and serve that created deity, fed by their hardened hands.
We both love the addiction
and wish to leave it,
shoving Copenhagen on a rotten tooth.

01 DECEMBER 2005

Remember, young man,
God mocks all our plans
we make in our peace and our pride,

for on this bright day
He took me away
with IED straight to His side.

A PRAYER BEFORE MISSION

Brace my mortal man's heart, oh God.
Steel the contentious fears and passions
of my black and blue embattled soul.
Bid me fling timid emotion,
belched as from a cannon
over distant, unfound horizon.
Enflame sinew and muscle with potency and influence,
bones and tendons shored up for task at hand.
Lend swiftness to sharpened eyes
with razor aim by abrupt, unshaken hands.
Let me roar the songs of life and death
in blended celebration of both.
Fortify brothers mine the same,
engorging minds with breakneck power and joy
behind mask-like painted faces.
> *Lead me to the fray*
> *once more, my God, I pray!*

But now ends the time for prayer,
as violent battle dawns anew
under a splendid, wicked moonlight.

WARNED ME

They warned me of death,
and war's evil endeavor,
but nobody told me
we'd chase it forever.

MENTAL CONDITIONING

The first bloody thirst
gave way to the worst of us,
and minds, over time,
made that hatred sublime in us.

FATALLY FUNNELED

Despise this modernity,
its lack of necessity,
that drive entire meaning from man's lonely life.

The fatally funneled
in civility's tunnel
have lost the pure wildness of struggle and strife.

Pure feasting is shallow
if creation is fallow;
the crux there to conquer, to live and to die.

Cry no lament!
Keep soul unbowed, unbent!
An era of hard-handed men is well-nigh!

SHADES

Our countrymen look with their feigned interest high
 upon our long hist'ry of wars, both past and the nigh.
They see a checked board with its black and its white;
"Our" good and "Their" bad to divide in their sight.
The tribes and the beasts of our frayed foes' desires
surely contrast with these angels of ours!
But what if that checkerboard held no white knights,
no ivory pawns, the darkness to fight?
What if "Our" pieces were rather more red
from stomping the guts and the bones of the dead?
What if the pieces which protected you
were closer to darkness than ever you knew?

HELL-ARIOUS

They were my naysaying parade
of uneducated sages,
throwing bales of candied clichés.

They warned me of galling pain,
of starvation's chewing ache,
of endless weary days
and hate for the sake of hate.
"You'll catch the PTSD,
be a void hollow shell,
if you even return alive
from war's private hell!"

      Nobody thought to mention
      that it's hell-arious as well.

The chuckle of living
when others wish you dead,
the joy of being missed
as rounds snap by your head.
To savor a fresh Marlboro
as if it were your last
after killing a man neatly
five-hundred yards past.
No one told me of friends
like Natty and silly Billy;
the hilarious redneck
and the comic from Philly.
We put the "laughter" in "slaughter"
with knee-slapping jokes,
the dark gallows humor
each firefight would provoke.

Cover a man in ceramic and Kevlar,
seat him with rifle on combat's fell throne,
see him reduced to his truest domain;
a clown that is armed,
      wrapped in science and stone.

JUST PASSING THROUGH

In opiate night's breeze,
under opiate moon,
the basaltic net of the sky flung wide
 in colors of invisible spectrum . . .
Gritty flesh of urban setting
painted in optic green,
festive but for fell context . . .
Eight hardened men enter walls,
invading house in silent wave
through air thick, glutted
with scents and snores
of the sleeping, unaware,
drifted people.
Did they wake next morning,
complaining of dreams, of images rife
with malicious, night-seeing men
behind painted rifles?
Did our shades filter through
in chimera vision,
soft-footed
through labyrinthian sleeping form,
silent and unknown as
the shadows of ghosts?

NIGHT MISSION

We pause to gaze with crusted, rusty eyes
at the nonchalance of the crimson setting sun,
   a haunting beggar
     limping across the sky in shoes of blood,
     drowning in fire in an insane, incessant agony
     amidst a far-reaching desert quiet.

We watch in jaded voyeurism
   with steady hearts closed
   to beauty of unfeigned color,
waiting only for night's purpling door
   to shut upon us,
     to continue invisible patrol
       through briefly jeweled sands.

A man does not need light
to see in the black –
   he need only be open to the darkness.

TEAM PHOTO

Barons of battle,
gluttons of strife,
our mothers did vary,
yet brothers in pride.

Cocky and sure
of our dangerous blood.
Capable men
in a violent flood.

Imperial tools
in empire's grown trade
of honeycombed wars
and cellular raids.

Heathens, believers,
and rogues, we were clad
in unified purpose
and deeds grown quite mad.

One final image
for memory's sake
before we begin,
the earth there to shake.

THE NEWBIE

All Newbies want is to look like they're not
disquieted souls who hide their own fear.
With wide open eyes, they seek to fit in
by buying the costliest tactical gear.

The Newbie absorbs all the trappings of war,
adorning his flesh with black ink to appear
a soldier with reckless desire to fight,
though never set foot on that bloody frontier.

He'll strap forty mags to his chest and his back,
and twenty grenades at his pockets and rear,
with pouches and pouches and multicam pouches
and so much equipment he looks like a sphere.

But mock that poor "Newbie," or "Cherry," or "Boot"
at great risk to yourself with confident sneer.
Though lacking your knowledge, he wants to be part of
your militant gang he so highly reveres.

When courage has failed in the midst of the fight,
desire to prove oneself to his own peers
has carried men far in the push to become
a dependable fighter for brothers so dear.

THE OLD HAND

The Veteran has a fell look all his own,
a confidence boasting the passing of years,
with calmest demeanor though danger's at hand
and slit-narrowed eyes from life so severe.

Unconsciously competent, ever alert,
he commands with a roar and intent ever clear.
His instincts developed, his senses so sharp
that he'll sniff out an ambush in dead atmosphere.

Only what's needed adorns lethal frame;
some mags flat to body around trauma shears,
some tourniquets easily reached with each hand,
some water, some chow for a mission austere.

He's learned how to fight, survive, and to thrive.
He'll beg, borrow, steal, or perhaps commandeer
the things that he needs to accomplish the job.
His toughness is not just a mere thin veneer.

So Newbies, you listen to Veteran's voice
and do what he says with the utmost of cheer.
He'll teach you to live through the worst of the war.
His instructions are harsh, but deadly sincere.

OLD SCHOOL

The feral old man
holstered lightning pistol with leathered hands,
his teeth stained by curses of decades,
his arms by scars and ink
older even than me.
Sinewy of skill,
stalwart as a summer storm,
his mercenary eyes bespoke
a defiance incalculable.
Through a beef jerky grin his laugh cracked,
    "It's just snapping necks
       and cashing checks until lunch,"
exhaling Marlboro mist, black coffee breath,
    "then it's fast-roping
       and J-turns, my boy!"

CIVILIZATION AND STRIFE

(Originally published in
In Love... & War: The Anthology of Poet Warriors)

A dog bounced, yipping and yawping, clamoring for affections.
Fat of belly, soggy of flesh, and tender of feet,
though he was no longer a "he;" in gender a defeat.
Evolved and progressed, soft and voluminous,
he/it loudly consumed at "Vocif 'R Us,"
and lonely, clawlessly, shat out his slumberous soul.
"Civilization" was his name, a fevered pitch of ease.

The wild gave way to his slobbering bark, blown away
by his haughty enlightenment, reason and strength unheeded.
His claws were vestigial, his teeth removed, unneeded.
An endless maelstrom of directions, a wide road was his domain,
leading nowhere and nohow, widening into a plain.
Yet alone, he consumed in a storm of cowardice,
and courage was a curse to him.

Away from this fat spectre loped a pack.
Ancient and terrible, lean and functional, they ran,
in flares of grey, black, brown, and tan.
They too consumed, but garbage and leavings they did not scour.
They hunted, they tore, they shattered, and devoured.
As many, they ran as one, complete in function and form;
Effectual, advantageous, a study in terrible utility.

No worthless part was on their streamlined bodies,
 "Pretty" and "Soft" were their curses, "Beauty" as worthless a pledge.
A narrow path, a ray in math, thinned before them to a cutter's edge,
 "Red in Tooth and Claw" they were, stripped of voluptuous fat,
worshipping their gods with blood, gore, and violent habitat.
Their name was "Strife." Their name was "Power."
The fathers of all that makes men great.

FRAGO

Missions of this abrupt, disruptive nature
require abbreviated preparations.
No two-hour Concept of Operations,
No oxymoronic thousand-slide brief,
No terrain model made
        of yard, paint, sand,
        and Kindergarten skill.
Mags already loaded,
Rounds are in the chamber,
Radios crypto-filled,
Painted faces already fading
        from days in harsh dirt,
        growing a layer of caked,
        solid sweat and oil,
        with raw slurry in pits and groin.
Had we worn swords, blood would have stained
        with terrible paint,
        the hilts of our steel.
But rifles we carried to ply our trade,
        and only the smell of burnt carbon
        gave tale to our work.
The blanket of night surrounds senses
filtered by electronics,
sharpened by week's starvation.
We step not past a line,
        nor unto a breach.
We do not enter the fray.
We are already here.
We never left.

SIGNIFICANT MECHANISM OF INJURY

I gaze at the stars between my feet,
beautiful, silent, uncaring . . .
This, then, is my unrighteous end.

No life flashed before my eyes,
merely a wordless
?
followed by the ineloquent,
!

Undone, not by enemy's
soul-soaking violence,
but by the cruel coupling
of cliffs and gravity.

Resting, finally, at mountain's base,
it is not the last time I say,
"I should be feeling something,"
yet for once the sentiment
is about physical body alone.

DEAD BODY

Expectation was not met,
no grimaced face in pain, hard-set.
Absent too was sweet repose
in fresh dead bodies laid in rows.

and the radio squawks while attached to my chest
my heartbeat is fast though my body's at rest

Like a funeral I thought it'd be –
closed eyes, hands clasped, a look of peace.
It was nothing that sophisticated;
he was just a sack of skin deflated.

and the bullets snap by so close o'er my head
but time is now stopped as I stare at the dead

His jaw was slack and open wide.
It hung there slightly to the side.
Retracted back into his neck,
his head pulled back in C-spine wreck.

and my rifle hangs limp and forgotten at hand
as my mind starts to reel under war's harsh demand

Dirt caked eyes half wide and wet.
His hair was lank with grime and sweat.
His mouth was packed with rocks and sand
(he'd dropped face first to die unplanned).

and the screams of our wounded from enemy fire
are angry and deep, war's awful choir

His skin was wax from lack of blood.
It'd left his flesh, turned dust to mud.
Crimson, brick, they swirled around
in unmixed colors, paint profound.

and close air support is now dropped far away
the A-10's and fighters have come out to play

His wounds were meat, ground beef uncooked.
The rounds had hit his ribs and hooked.
They'd left his back far down below
and stolen chunks of bloody dough.

and the blasts from the bombs have dropped from on high
but the dead keep on staring straight up in the sky

His feet were bare and hard as horn,
his clothing riddled, stained and torn.
No body armor graced his chest;
just AK mags stitched in a vest.

and firefights suit my old teammate just fine
so he replies tersely from two-forty-nine

"Not a man!" my mind did scream.
A mannequin it surely seemed.
No muscle tone or body firm –
"Dead weight;" it's where we get the term.

and pictures are taken, for intel, I swear!
images held from that day over there

He'd fought us bravely til the end,
his Afghan village to defend.
I thank my God it's no Marine,
just man caught in the war machine.

PURPLE HEART

A medal I'm given one bleak desert day
for actions the contents of which I'm ashamed.
Vengeful sun blasts on our tan uniforms,
while horseflies attack leathered faces in swarms.

A heart made with purple, with gold, and with pain
was given to many in long human chain.
My scars are so small, but their echoes so vast;
shrapnel in knee, a bad infantry back,
numbness in thighs when I'm at parade rest,
and a name that is etched in the flesh on my chest.

The first that deployment, though far from the last
to earn that damn medal. Those numbers grew fast.

My thoughts, they go back to a ride on a plane;
the wounded to transport from vicious campaign.
We walked into cargo hold, waited to fly
on to Landstuhl, a hospital clear cross the sky.
We scuffled with nerves while settling in seats,
the pilots still making their pre-checks complete.
Then came the gurneys, those grave rolling beds,
and on them were soldiers, Marines halfway dead.
Unconscious and limbless, with bandages tight,
IVs and blessed morphine to bleed out their fight.
Their silent repose was as loud as a bomb,
their agony felt in pale faces so calm.
I don't deserve to be on the same plane as
these mangled men chemically fighting their pain.

Hear me! Forgive me for trespassing here!
This place, it is sacred! Your wounds do endear
it to man and to God with your sacrificed blood
that spilled in contested Afghanistan mud.

They did not once move on that terrible ride,
condemning us all in our shame justified.

I'm back in formation, I'm standing in line
on ground that is hallowed in infantry shrine.
Beside me is Murphy, with seams on his face
from shrapnel, from fighting at feverish pace in
curst Musah Qualéh, where an RPG blast
went off in a firefight, branding him fast.
Yet ever the fighter, he got up and poured out
his hate with his rifle on Taliban horde.
Thought five-foot, nine inches, he stood so much taller
than many of us, his great brav'ry enthralled us.

They gave me the medal, the same as that man
and poor bastards on plane ride from Afghanistan.
"Congrats on your medal," said family and friends,
but I know the truth that will ever ascend
in my mind that my God in His ever-great grace
allowed me to walk with a faltering pace
with these giants of courage and sacrifice true;
an honor and privilege that's known by so few.

THE STONED OLD MAN

He welcomed us happily
giddy with rotted grin
and wind-withered arms
his hair and ancient beard
colored as soiled bed sheets
his vacant eyes red as the dawn

Beside our rushed admonition
huddling family hid in terror
women
children
small young men
waiting for death to follow fear

Smiling
        nodding
                giggling
The Stoned Old Man
affirmed our dire warning . . .
and shrugged castle spire shoulders

The first of the bombs
from our own friendly side
screamed down to us all
shattered tank-proof walls
turned air to bitter ash
Still The Stoned Old Man stood
smiling
        nodding
                giggling
by his five-leaved crops
laughing in red-eyed defiance
of burning world and mortal fear

FROM THE TOWER

From the coffin of the tower I see the city
Mantled in the grey blur of the dawn.
The early lights scintillate like glitter abundant,
spread over the ancient turd of a country
languishing on the dry plains.

From the steel tower I smell the rain
gulped by the thirsty weak soil.
The moon dust rises with each drop
like a miniature mortar round of water.
Sewage backs up, diseased garbage
blooms its assaulting, invigorated stench.

From the silence of the tower I hear the flies
droning in search of wretchedness.
Recklessly launching their raisin bodies
on glass, steel, and faces.

From the oven of the tower I feel
the blistering breeze baking my core.
"A dry heat" may be fine for some,
 but blow dryers are distressing companions
when aimed at the face
for eight cheerless hours.

From the heights of the tower I taste the dust.
Fecal in composition, it clings to the air;
a vaporous sloth of disease and shit.
With each breath it stains my lungs,
becoming a part of me, my blood, my bones.

FACETS OF DYING

You think of death as terrible,
an ending of a soul.
but is there frightful fulfillment
in dark reaper's glow?

MAINLY VICE

I cough my vice from calloused lungs
expectorate from dip-raped gums
to revel in substance's domain
is worship of our fancied chains

EATING MRE'S

I hear there's no preservatives.
They never taste *too* bad,
but after weeks, I need no toilet,
just some wipes and a baseball bat

GOD BLESS THOSE HEATHEN BOYS

(Originally published in
In Love... &War: The Anthology of Poet Warriors)

God, bless those heathen boys
they who worship you not,
for they are forever my brothers,
and spilled crimson blood is our lot.

Lord, bless those heathen boys,
the best men I'll ever know,
who have fought Them and They
in sea, in sand, in snow.

Father, save those heathen boys,
they who carry the sword.
They give their sweat, their hearts, their lives,
all more than they can afford.

Jesus, take care of those heathen boys
who worship with wine and beer.
They drink to remember song, to laugh,
and to wholly forget their fear.

Creator, bless those heathen boys
who take women for a night of pleasure.
Their time is short and brutal on earth,
filled with pain without measure.

Sovereign, save those heathen boys,
forced to drink the cup of hate and rage,
for they must survive their world of war,
they are fed death, and blood is their wage.

Spirit, watch over those heathen boys,
though they have their vices and sins,
For the best Christians aren't perfect.
We all fight the savage within.

Christ, take in those heathen boys,
for they are without a home.
They return from war changed and scarred,
and in their own nation they restlessly roam.

NOW IS THE HOUR OF COMBAT'S RED FIRE

Now is the hour of combat's red fire
A river of life that is ended in full
Forever we bleed on the altar of fate
Enslaved by the might of war's powerful pull

Facing the wrath of the cavalry's charge
and claiming that victory mentally wrought,
battl'ng the cowardice drowning our souls
for all that we've done and all that we ought

Faces of living and bravery one,
we stand at the gates of our savagery bold.
Peering through hell and then finding it sane,
the image of strife that is desp'rate and old.

Withstanding the nature of warlike mankind
is not in our fate to be darkly foreseen.
Rather we throw ourselves into the fray
locking and loading as death-bound machines.

THE OVER-DRAMATIC PRIVATE

I entered the Corps a young boy,
my flesh plumped with unabated life.
Hardship I thought I'd known at the hands
of drill and combat instructors,
but I'd not yet known the shattering wrath of the Squad Leader.
The screaming giants ruled the millimeters of existence
with the law of the fist,
demanding steel from my clammy, sweaty soul.
They cursed my weakness, those men with a countenance
leathered by the desert-dry blasts of hate.
They cursed my frailty with words like maces,
elaborate verses like swords wrought in combat.
They told me of their grim, black war,
and sang the songs of iron and slaughter.
My timid irises widened in wonder
as I listened, open-mouthed with staccato breath
to their tales of killing and dying
in the soils of Iraq perfumed with palms
and shrapnel;
that place where fear flew like ragged pennants
torn in a swift-rising wind.
Our fated departure to war sent beach waves of terror
shuddering through my spine,
my heart was a house fragranced with piss,
the whites of my eyes widened as sheets,
the panicked entreaties of prey amid the hunt.
Yet the ancestry of my animal brain
and the call of my God invited, yes, demanded courage
to evolve and create myself anew.
Forward I had to march on hardening feet,
forward to drive on detonating roads,
forward to ride in creaking turrets,
and forward the sinews of my life lengthened and strengthened
until the fat of ease was boiled from my bones,
and I became like them,
and one of them.

PUT DOWN YOUR STEEL

I awoke as a Roman, burning with ambition and vigor.
My spear and shield were my glory and way of life.
Mighty Carthage and Judah fell before me,
and now blue painted Celts fight naked in snow and mud.
From the northern woods a voice calls to me;
"Put down your steel, young warrior,
for there is much life left to live!"
"I will not!"
I roar with rage, I call with drive,
"For my work is not yet done!
I have yet to conquer all,
I've only now begun!"

I awoke as a knight with mail, mace, and horse,
my sword a sharp glinting cross for the glory of God.
Brave Saracens and terrible Mongols
mixed their worthy blood on my blade.
In the mountains I hear a cry in the wind;
"Put down your steel, brave warrior,
for there is much life left to live!"
"I shall not,"
I sound with manly voice, all the bedlam I had to give,
"For my war is not yet done!
Danger strikes my land
and my people stand alone!"

I awoke a privateer with restless and guilty heart,
wielding cutlass, cannon, and the might of the crown.
I plundered and ravaged for profit
and the fear from men seeing my treacherous black flag.
From across the sea I feel the voice again;
"Put down your steel, vicious warrior,
for there is much life left to live!"
"I will not,"
I laugh with sadness for men I've deprived.
"For my war is yet underway!
Someday I will not need my sword,
and I long for that day."

I awoke in the GWOT with tattoos, dip, and gun.
Rifle, pistol, radio and bombs
were the irreverent tools of my deadly trade.
My list of enemies grown vast and diverse,
global foes both worthy and not.
As I slumber in sand I hear the near voice;
"Put down your steel, old warrior,
for short is the life left to live!"
"I cannot,"
I whispered tearless and cold, desp'rate to survive,
"My rifle is here to stay.
Without it, I am nothing,
I know no other way."

A SONG OF INFANTRY
(Inspired by Walt Whitman's "A Song of Joys")

-0300-
Oh to be once more an infantryman!
The release of a ruck after a murderous hike,
to feel the air upon blistered feet,
knowing my aches and breed are pinnacles!
To take pride in pain, severe bliss in sleepless starvation,
to store up for myself brothers in Heaven,
carrying the weight of the steel and the blood
in a laugh that is aimed at Death by my side

-0311-
Oh to know the pride of a RifleMan,
that melding of two treasured terms in danger!
To have my arms, back and feet, my eyes and my soul
hardened forever by life's violent means.
To kick in doors, flashbang in hand;
a maelstrom of sound and the light fantastic!
The cornerstone of Corps and Army alike,
where the fulcrum is of fire, granite, and might.

-0317-
Oh, the glory of the sniper, that hunter of gunmen!
To be the poet of Death and the singer of fear,
sending choruses in a copper-coated coloratura!
To be a master of prey and seeing unseen,
as slow and sure as a disease yet unborn,
as deadly and accurate as a viper's wet grasp.
Be the grass, be the sand, be the trees wet with clinging rain,
suffering silently in the red hope of the finale of souls.

-0321-
Oh, the terrible honor of reconnaissance!
To be the envy of the Corps and its target at once!
Steel thy hearts, dear friends, dear assassins,
for the front lines are far behind you.
Take speed without sound and kill without feeling!
Be the cutting edge, the slipped blade in the heart,
our eyes and our daggers in the blackest of night!

-0331-
Oh, the joy of a machinegun in the shoulder!
Emotion emancipated in a wasp cloud of lead,
pouring out hatred like molten release.
To charge the handle with vigorous paw
and roar, "GUNS UP!" before mowing in droves.
Trace now with crimson's raw beam o'er fields
rich with targets made to absorb Marine wrath!

-0341-
Oh, the swagger of the mortarman!
The mad, wild math of death in flight,
the terrible geometry of jagged curves and shrapnel!
Launching blows from static rest,
over hills, behind walls, in trenches thought secure.
A terrible bell of both iron and pain,
drum firing with staccato embrace!

-0351-
Oh, the deafening labor of the assaultman,
that husbandry of the missile's legacy!
To plow battlefields with terrible tillage
with blast shattering time and mind!
To melt steel in hyperthermic candelabra,
leaving behind a famine of air,
a graveyard bereft of red atmosphere.

Our flesh is drained of superfluous waste,
our eyes narrowed by the blinding dark.
Our blood is viscous and vicious,
Our shoulders hunched, our jaws set.
We are friends of war!
We are known by combat!
We are partners with pain!
"Death, where is thy sting?"
We answer with wavelike chorus –
"In our hands, and our enemies' alike,
we deal and greet Death with equal familiarity."

THE HIDE

I found not that perfect hide,
that primordial hut dappled by verdant leaves
and flecked by discriminate sun,
which deigned to cover us in shadows random,
        ourselves ghosts of such shades.

Discovered by a brother, who even now
lay poised upon rooftop,
invisible even to me.
Cushioned from IDF and HIMARs by its
        solitary distance,
nevertheless attracting adversarial actions.

Insignificant shack sat rooted, unperturbed
by native disobedience or imperial punishment.
Unshackled of blatant presence,
it trod that narrow beam between
        obvious and oblivion.

But for the chirping of radio chatter,
silence hung heavily here, exacerbating the
        wild loneliness,
suspending the moment in nameless unremembrance.

Its unquenched beauty lay not in
pastel colors or shapely geometry,
        but rude, vulgar utility;
foreground matching backdrop,
concealing hazardous intent,
Walls thick with brick, mud, and straw,
protecting blood and brain from
        vigorous enemy.

An oasis in a pressurized zoo
housing predators free to hunt
with eyes terrible and cunning,
discerning and hooded,
exploring unwitting targets as
        orbic constellations.

LEFTOVERS

In the moon dust it lay,
relaxed and wet, soft and wet,
tinged grey in tan sand,
the piece of brain (of mind) lay without thought.
Drag marks furrowed shallow earth,
his body dragged, tugged away.
"You forgot something!"
I want to say.
Whose bullet expanded his mind?
What was held in this piece of man?
His language center?
A memory of his beloved mother's cooking?
His immortal soul?
No, I have it!
It surely held his hatred for America,
and we've cured him
with 7.62-millimeter lobotomy.

HYPOCRISY

We destabilize nations with 1st World predations
    while civilization complains of creation
of terrorist cells in the pitiful hellscape
    where hatred wells up, but AFN tells us
"Wear glowbelts and masks!" but never to ask
    if our missions and tasks are outclassed and surpassed
by farmers of dirt who stood up and cursed us
    for bloodthirsty ways in the land we've coerced.

PITY

I've never seen Iraqis mope,
or Afghans shuffle feet and whimper.
There's something to be said
for living in a land
where no one tells you you're a victim.

WHAT WERE WE

What were we, but analogue solutions
to digital problems in fugitive states?
Our youthful obscurity used in factory formation,
the concealed breeding of convulsions of hate,
forever frothing that poisonous weakness
disguised as a broken, hopeful fate.

THE PURE WARRIOR

He belonged to a past hideous,
a midnight of time and living stone
with science and modernity a whispered hope
of dawn in hours of millennia.

The grain of his tissue crossed and hatched;
to peace, he was perpendicular.
In times of rest, he raged.
In eras of ease, he paced,
settled only by the promise of blood
and the love of the battle axe.

Repose was atrophy to his predator limbs,
a tomb of plenty and prosperity.
Buried 'neath layers of treacled melody,
he bristled and ground in softening light.
His shivering soul consumed his flesh;
a sword in a sleeping stream,
made to thrust,
        left to rust.

ASK ME NOW

Ask me now, brother,
here in the air-conditioned barracks,
with beer in hand, cigarettes in lips,
blasting AC/DC in still, dry air.
Ask me now.

I'll promise the vow to you,
made in countless wars in ages past.
Pinky swear? Hell yes, I'll pinky swear.
Here in the peace before violence,
I'll swear to you.

Bullet holes, abdominal wounds,
missing limbs, mangled faces,
all can be discounted in comparison to the ultimate shame,
that wound all men fear above all;
losing genitals in horrid blasts, wretched fire.

I promise you if you promise me,
I'll kill you if you'll kill me.
Shoot me in the head or heart,
it matters not which.
Just make sure I'm gone, brother.
We both shudder in fear of losing
that most precious part of our flesh,
so ask me now, here in the calm,
while liquid courage yet runs in my veins.

You say that others have promised,
that battle buddies are already sworn
in fearful betrothal?
Smith and Martinez?
O'Neil and Malcolm?
Richardson and Schmidt?
Very well, you and I will swear,
but ask me now, brother.

Ask me now, here, today,
before the metal hits the meat,
before I skid up to your prone body
to hear whimpers of agony.
Ask me now before I have to see
pleading eyes brimming with fear,
asking, "Am I ok... *down there?*"

Ask me now before I have to check,
removing armor and trousers,
hands slick with bloody glue.
Before I have to draw unwanted pistol,
placing under quivering chin.
Ask me now, brother.

Don't ask me then.

THE [COWARD] LEADER

His watery heart may bide time
with iron countenance.
Afraid, not of enemy's face,
but rather of underlings' scorn,
he lashed his fear upon surrounding men
in vapid, unnecessary strokes.
"If I fail, the scorn of my betters
will stain my [yellow] soul!
To show my power, I must loose my ire,
making a plumage of my wrath!"
Seeking only popularity,
he curried favor [to all but his own],
shutting down initiative and thought
with [know-it-all] pride.
"It's not my idea, it must be wrong!"
Complaining [incessantly] to all open ears,
he moaned to the forgetful sky
of the incompetence of his men
[in reflection of himself].

THE (ABRIDGED) AFGHAN

Look ye, on the Afghan! In harshest land he throve!
From sand he'd raise his poppies; from rocks, his stanky weed grove!
(how he fought us drugged and stoned, the good Lord only knows!)

Marvel at the Afghan! His kingdom made of stones!
The tunnels were his castle halls, his subjects; Russian bones.
(how he fought them before Stingers, good Lord only knows!)

Be amazed at the Afghan! He is an army's woe;
Invaders broke upon his lands, and empires overthrown!
(how many mighty nations died, good Lord only knows!)

Thank God for the Afghan; the bitterest of foes
that thrive in the deserts and mountains capped in snow!
(how they live without water, good Lord only knows!)

Thank God for the Afghan! Poor bastards died in droves,
attacked in pairs, tens, and hundreds; from the very rocks he would grow!
(how many we killed, good Lord only knows!)

Thank God for the Afghan! He gave us quite a show!
A helluva fight was all we asked, and he never did forgo!
(how we'll live without this foe, good Lord only knows!)

AFGHAN NIGHTS

The cool wind envelopes,
covering whispers of murder –
soft ice in a glass of poison.
The sand in this place,
       ancient and paled by eons,
is ground to a knowing dust
uncaring of the hands of time.
Does it disdain the touch of my feet;
an infant crawling on the graves of nations?

Poems of Life

SONG OF LIFE

The Song of Life is the more arduous tune,
for it does not imprint or stain the heart.
Peace is not a spontaneous thing,
it must be sought with gasping breath
as with a distant horizon.
Far simpler to dirty the soul with blood . . .
nigh impossible to wipe it off.
The goal is worthy, nonetheless,
even if never attained,
for the ones surrounding you in this race
 are the things of God.

AUTUMN INDIANA DRIVE

There is life in this clay,
a breath deep and cleansing.

A slow drive with windows down
drinks in the new cold air.
I smell the faraway smoke of
dried maple and leaves.
It is its own flavor on this slow, cold day.
There is no empty noise of pointless bustle,
no awful rush.
The silence is full, lonely and lovely.
It covers me and absorbs anxiety; a lovely gauze.

The *chuff* of the train on its tracks meets the air,
and the random squirrels rustle in the drowsy detritus.
Fallen leaves are a blanket of fire,
mild and golden.
They nestle the earth in its bed
before winter's taciturn arrival.

Flannel and Carhartt adorn me more fully
than the kingliest array.
My coat is a royal robe, my beanie a diadem.
The tender chill on my ruddy face
reminds me of the soothing warmth in my comforted frame.

A covered bridge dawns on the horizon,
bathed in a deep red, ancient and peeling.
Its creaks are the respirations of a living thing . . .
prescient,
content,
a grandfather taking his repose and stroking his beard.

My wife at my side pleasantly chats
of holidays and presents.
My children laugh and fight in their new
and uncontrolled vitality.

The forests and fields of Indiana –
they are a near heaven.
They are a drink of peace.

FINALLY HOME

The tension bleeds through arteries trembling
walls dilated from peace.
Glad returning hugs, kisses
work healing magic of Narnian air.
Neither intravenous caffeine
nor a carton of cowboy killers
could keep me awake.
Real sleep draws me in
a slumber so deep
a hellish trip was nearly worth
arrival at home.

THE THIRD DAY

His life was a bared throat,
an unending dare.
He passed bruised reeds yet unbroken,
smoking wicks glowing still.
A peace of drowsing breezes
and of dormant meadows was His wake,
yet wounded was His magnificence,
marred by baleful stripes on loving flesh.
The squalling wind lashing
at naked sacrifice
echoed a death-march on convulsive earth,
the floating spires of cross-nailed agony
were but lathes carving us to gleaming glory.
He, a wight, a blight in eyes of God,
cast our sins into pit of ceaseless perturbity.
Sins! Now mere tyrants shivering in caves!
Death was not His autumnal outcome,
but His vanquished enemy,
lured by unseen power,
crushed by the Son of Man.

HOOSIER BLONDE

Her beauty first struck me in faraway college.
I creepily stared and then I acknowledged
that in all of that city,
there was none quite so pretty
as that beautiful, blue-eyed, Hoosier blonde.

She is the proof that our Father loves me
and wishes my heart to be happy and free.
And above all the world,
I love that sweet girl . . .
that beautiful, blue-eyed, Hoosier blonde.

For years she was married to me and the Corps,
but something was missing! There had to be more!
So she gave me a smile
and then our first child!
A beautiful, blue-eyed, Hoosier blonde.

A second! A third! Three sweet little girls,
each dimpled and cute with long golden curls!
And my wife was the source
of their beauty, of course;
those beautiful, blue-eyed, Hoosier blondes.

But then we did leave the "safe" military;
She was a mother, I a "mercenary,"
and while I was gone,
she gave me a son,
that beautiful, blue-eyed, Hoosier blonde.

My soul and my heart in her loving, kind hands,
she has my whole body, every sinew and strand.
The pride of my life
is her as my wife,
that beautiful, blue-eyed, Hoosier blonde.

LET MY FAITH BE BOLD AND WILD

Let my faith be bold and wild,
        alive with steel and blood-red fire.
Truth of God in heart and mind
        His Word forever real entire

Let it writhe and breathe my soul,
        a sword of God in darkness vast.
It must work today forthwith
        to bring to life Your deeds long past.

Let my faith take action full,
        a life of pray'r for Heaven's grace.
Daily rendr'ing worship's song
        to learn our place in earthly race.

Let it drive into my heart,
        like blade in joints and marrow splits,
steering every deed and rule,
        to Thy will daily commit

METAPHORS

(Originally published in
In Love… &War: The Anthology of Poet Warriors)

Oh, false world, fill your pages with comparisons,
Your thin papers with metaphors!
Let my life be real, a thick and tangible thing,
Drinking of the rich blood of actuality!

More than "like" or "as,"
More than airy ink on featureless paper.
Let the ink be puckered scars and experience,
my soul and flesh the searing pages.

Banish from me the easy lies,
smoke and similes sweet to the mind.
Those mere mirrors of lost chance
pouring through limp, untested fingers.

Give me more than coffeehouse prose,
that decaf Chicken Soup for the Gutless.
Throw me to the wolves and beasts!
Let me fight, bite, test my might!

Let shallow movies not define my Love,
those platforms of simple fuckery.
Let me find naked flesh and mortal bone,
And skin electric worth memorizing.

Let me create a roaring life with my Love,
With a kiss, a moan, and a sigh
To contrast against the pale, bleak, and
disguised meaninglessness.

Let that Life bound outward
Giggling, growing, leaping
with the control of a sprinting bonfire
On a dry September day!

Give me Battle and wild War,
For the sake of the barbaric fight!
Politics and vomitous reasons be damned,
Like the yellow First World contests and bouts.

Let me feel the voluptuous red, hear the blood,
Roaring through arteries stretched to snapping,
leaving behind delights and woes
Too light, relaxed, and sweet for a warrior's stomach.

"My struggle is like a war,"
They simper over iPhones and running water,
While I am gifted bone, blood, bayonet, and bullets
To Fight, and Fight against, in the foreign dirt.

Let my God be found real and full,
Untamed, worthy of fierce worship!
Let the weak deities fade and die,
Blown by the vitreous smoke of His passing!

Give me surety of His strength, might,
and judgement, tempered with mercy
A God worth trembling before
Rather than guessing at.

Let me find Brotherhood!
Let me be needed in the fevered mud,
So my arms will not be empty, idle.
I carry and am likewise carried.

Let my Brothers be an unrivaled rivalry,
No mere boys' club.
We chant the songs of strength!
We Fight the songs of youth!

Prodigals, killers, dilated braggards,
They mean more than placid acquaintances.
Emptied of Self, my Brothers selflessly bear
My weight and soul, and I Theirs.

Some men by metaphors do not live,
Or scrape about with cheap imitations.
They find Strength for their Strife,
And seek Strife for the Strength.

Their life is distilled in pure vitality
Who love their Women, bring forth
a Child, seek a Fight, serve their God,
and adopt Brothers with blood-soaked arms.

FIRST WORLD PROBLEMS

There was a small man that world's nature abhorred.
His life was a curse to mankind and our Lord.
Existence a squander of blessings that poured out on
him in unearnéd reward.
He sat on his ass, complaining of boredom
though never quite working, a concept deplored.
A worthless life spent, ev'ry comfort to hoard,
but ever his body and mind unexplored.
A complacent man, cowardly, simp'ring toward
a life and death passive, dark evil's own ward.
What gifts he did waste of his own dead accord
while resting, forever unsung and ignored!

THE POET
(dedicated to the new poets emerging from the GWOT)

His writing is a ghillie
of burlap and feathered grass,
a reined control of chaos
wrapped in violence ecstatic.
Water with whiskey
and mescaline to grow
a twisted art of truth,
complex and beautiful,
with flecks of loving design.

Nature abhors straight lines and rhymes,
making same sound time after time,
but his design, soaked in wine, reads perfectly fine.

MONGRELS

They're iron ore, all gravel and hardness,
like cheerios hardened into baking car seat.
These mongrel dogs, made of sand and dust,
blood scratching through dried veins;
they crawl, slinking with heads bowed
and rock eyes wary.
Mere clawed snakes with fur,
despised, diseased, starving,
wretched and lowly,
yet even these birth beautiful pups.
Of what, then, are we capable?

MY FOREST

I
travel
through trails
unseen through thorn
and thicket, unknown but to ants
and white-bellied deer.
I wrap myself in leaves, I blanket my
man's scent with bark and wild, wild wind.
I hover in the woods, alone and surrounded by soil
unknown to human foot and boot.
My senses, they animate to voluptuous tones of existence;
Harken the trees, well-nigh awake,
whispering in cloistered alcoves, a choir of ancient priests, hands
exalted and exalting.
I smell the cold itself in snapping air; it is the scent of frost, of
blue, piercing hues.
Squirrels, red and gray and cowardly of soul sing the songs of
hunger and octaved gossip.
The scent,
the sight,
the sound,
the spirit
is that of caution,
a breath held in anticipation.

HER

Be my easy truth, my point of
gravitational navigation
in my free-floating struggle of strain.
Be a stealth magnetic to my ferrous core,
make me thy escape, thy fire-worked reality.
Be not my God, my titanic deity,
but my tender altar;
Upon thee I lay my spirit,
        my self,
                my sacrifice. . .
Cry to me as I to thee
in essence intertwined and become one.

MY SON

(Originally published in
In Love... &War: The Anthology of Poet Warriors)

Be strong, my son. Be strong.
Let your arms not forsake work,
let your back not forget weight.
Make your muscles hard and hungry,
your spine unyielding and straight.
Let hardness be your trait!
Be strong, my son. Be strong,
for I am your father,
and the Lord is your God!

Be brave, my boy. Be brave.
Leave the ways of the coward,
be the one called "Bold!"
In desperate times, be the measure,
though times are bleak and cold.
Be courageous to behold!
Be brave, my son. Be brave,
for I am your father,
and the Lord is your God!

Be honorable, my lad. Be honorable.
Abide by the code of your tribe,
from your men earn only respect!
Show your worth to your brothers,
let threats fear your group, and redirect.
Their values you should perfectly reflect!
Be honorable, my lad. Be honorable,
for I am your father,
and the Lord is your God!

Be skillful, my child. Be skillful.
Let your handiwork have merit,
lend worth to your trade.
Let your calloused hands use tools,
a hammer, nails, a blade.
Let them marvel at what you have made!
Be skillful, my child. Be skillful,
for I am your father,
and the Lord is your God!

(continue)

Be dangerous, little warrior. Be dangerous.
No man is good who is also weak,
nor does merit come from the willful frail.
Let your arms be a mighty wind,
your mind a fearless gale.
Let strife make you prevail!
Be dangerous, little warrior. Be dangerous,
for I am your father,
and the Lord is your God!

Be loving, little man. Be loving.
Let your wife know your heart,
your children your tender embrace.
Show devotion to your family,
let them see God's grace.
Your fondness should be commonplace!
Be loving, little man. Be loving,
for I am your father,
and the Lord is your God!

Be honest, my heir. Be honest.
Say what you will do.
Do what you will say.
Tell the truth despite the consequences,
as long as it is called "Today."
Do it daily, come what may!
Be honest, my heir. Be honest,
for I am your father,
and the Lord is your God!

Be holy, young one. Be holy.
Study the Scriptures,
and learn the ways of God.
Control your passions and desires,
and choose the right path to trod.
Be more than just a righteous façade!
Be holy, young one. Be holy,
For I am your father,
and the Lord is your God!

Be wise, little friend, be wise.
Read the books and learn the facts,
the history, the math, the science.
Do not be dull and stupid,
or on simple thoughts place your reliance!
Against foolishness scream your defiance!
Be wise, little friend. Be wise,
for I am your father,
and the Lord is your God!

Be better, my son. Be better.
Many sins have I committed,
many mistakes have I made.
Learn from my many faults.
avoid the prices I have paid.
Do not be afraid to
Be better, my son. Be better
even more than your father,
for the Lord is your God!

SOCIAL MEDIA

Emasculated masturbation
with keyboard in hand
grand deeds of sand
for vain brand loyalty.
a like,
a lie,
with canned response
of bland impact.
"I create change and take a stand!
Submit to my demands for this,
our nation grand,
our tortured, divided land!"
Time online, enacting plans,
but few really understand that
it's all fake pixels secondhand.

OLD DEPLOYMENT BIBLE

A deployment gift, I stole it for free
from a chapel in that dusty FOB,
and carried it everywhen and everywhere
for blessings and edification.
The years carved themselves upon the yielding gray
cover stained with spilled coffee
and Copenhagen-darkened fingers,
the pages with ink and tears.
Not a venerated monolith or unused idol,
I carelessly tossed in pocket, suitcase, and ruck.
It is an old friend made dear from use;
a Velveteen Rabbit of paper and print.
Highlighters, pens, and pencils have lined,
questioned,
digressed,
transgressed on its sacred text.
Excited or sleepy hands tore seams and corners.
Idle folding fingers turned posterboard cover
to leather-like softness.
From country to country,
airport to church,
pulpit to pew,
war-torn land to peaceful home,
it has accompanied me.
Questions answered,
answers questioned . . .
but the truth of the world was made a solid,
tangible thing;
Word of God forged handheld and accessible.
Like a wife or brother, it comforts
as it convicts and exhorts.
Ideas mocked by loved but hardened brothers
made all the more precious for
their controversy,
their audacity.
Verbs, adjectives, nouns, commands
reach from before time
through space
to captivate my eyes,
my mind,
my heart.

PLANT A GARDEN, YOUNG WARRIOR

Plant a garden, young warrior,
from the finest of seeds!
Swiftly! While life beats in your breast!
Be worthy of their fruit,
and do not neglect your duty,
for you are a man!
Take a sainted wife, father vibrant children!
Be worthy of both,
for to neglect life is futility,
a chasing of death,
and a waste of your fighting soul.

COWBOY DREAM

Harmonica is caught by desert wind,
    and stars twinkle in ancient dance.
Flickered light blinks on rifle,
    on sunburnt skin and fallow sands.
A cowboy dream drifts in and out
    of resting evening's rustic tune,
shoehorned into modern vision
    by ancient nomadic boon.
Stars are seen through dual night tubes,
    swift winds blow through pickup tires.
They mix their winks with infrared
    in place of cheery cowboy fires.

PEACE OR COMFORT

Deny yourself comfort, my children,
both of body and of soul,
and so stiffen your developing minds and bones.
Comfort is not peace, but a different spectrum entirely.
The latter earned by strength exerted,
while the former is a drug,
an opiate of mindless fever.
Peace is the reward of struggle and strife,
a boon to men and warriors,
while comfort makes cowards of our heroes,
no more than time robbed from the pillars of greatness.
Peace is growth, a deep rest to strengthen
arms and back for challenges yet unmet.
A life of ease, my young precious ones,
does no more than beget a weak spirit.
When hardships arise, such men
will shake fists at God and universe,
cursing unfairness for a lack of spine.

FIRE

Stoke the flame, young self,
blinding and white though it may be now.
The feeding, the breathing of life
in those jagged, popping coals . . .
Should it die,
oh unfortunate, negligent boy,
it will suffer from your failure,
and yours alone.
Nourish with tender tinder,
love with kind kindling,
blossom into melting beauty,
and in the future cold, even the glowing embers
will warm you in your ancient years.

THROW ME TO THE FRAY

Throw me to the fray,
I cry of my God.
Strip bare the visceral
and expose my weakness to the Son.
Let me conquer self in Your Name,
and honor You with blinding purpose.

I must seek legitimacy for action,
and eschew superfluous thought;
the richness of ease and metaphorical being.
Give my spine steel, and my soul a supple strength
with which I may reach the fallen.

COMPRESSION

I dwelt in a city of culture and thought
and heavenly flavors on layers of rot;
    absorbed stimulation,
    infected radiation,
the finest my money could ever have bought.

I trekked to the deserts of bullets and dust
and violent men defined by distrust;
    its lack of compression
    created meditation,
and ink flowed to paper in life songs robust.

Why do the words thus in nature flow forth
in more rhythms and rhymes than ever before?
    No gripping sedation
    of metro predation,
but the winds and the sun and the breakings of war.

Its opiate is blinding, a weight
keeping you in bed
until weakness creates sores
weeping away your manly virility.

Addict your heart to pursuit! To action!
Leave forever the vice of the eyes,
the chains of images
which turn your man's heart
to a timid, simpering, Gollumn.
Feed not a wolf with sugared treats,
with unsatisfying, lifeless snacks.
Watch him run! Hunt!
See him chase his desire, and call it blessed.

Do not permit your wild heart
to be so easily fed,
so weakly sated,
a man and husband ineffectual, replaceable.

#49

A flower grows on a battlefield,
the stained residue of departed souls.
Caught in a rooted network,
buffeted by well-salted soil.
In violent, violet rivulets
she reached for the sun,
stretching petals to find me
amongst the bodies and the mud.

MALACHI

Dare I give or try to live of less than all I own?
Dishonor is a wretched visual; a soul of stone.
The ground must shake with all the weight of given flesh and bone
I hurl above the ones I love to fall to depths unknown.

WHEN IS A SUNSET LITTLE MORE

When is a sunset little more
than a sunset alone?
Can a bird simply be?
Can a rose merely be a plant in bloom?
A search for deeper meaning;
to folly it can lead.

We assign wonder to the rocks and trees,
wrapping them in metaphor.
"It is so like my version
of the universe I created!"
we say in wonder manufactured,
amazed at our own deepness of thought.

Yet sometimes a sunset is just the earth turning.
A bird is nothing more than itself.
A rose is a colorful bush.

Such things are precious in and of themselves.

To hold such a thing in your hand
and do nothing more than
let it be,
this is deep enough for a soul.

These are created things with purpose,
and we can be present in their company,
wondering at nothing
but their existence and creation.

DAUGHTERS

Winsome daughters,
with eyes of sable, sky, and sea,
from the heights of my love for you
we gaze down at the sapphire earth,
the waning moon,
the gilded sun.

In each of your faces familiar and dear
is the genius of the artists
and the poetry of the psalmist.
In you is the athletic joy of summers,
the giggle of a happy stream,
the dancing of autumn's falling leaves,
rambling,
spinning,
drifting in errant air.

I behold my girls
after long, dark days of toil.
Your loving countenances are a worthier visage
to weary father's eyes,
an arbor,
a harbor untouched
by world's stained hands.

War not with each other,
and so offend beauty and grace.
Know the rest-like peace,
the stuff of deepest dreams
lest frown cross maiden faces.

When years you reach
so dreadfully near
to leave our lovely dell
and dwell in harsh world's domain
with ache of heart and sore sorrow,
the haven of *father* will be
your lullaby refuge forever,
in home and in my open heart.

WEARY SMILE

I see you, preacher, standing there
with your weary, shiny smile.
The weight of God is on your shoulders
and you've not rested in a while.
You're holding it together,
but feel you're by yourself.
There's no friends except on Sundays.
During the week you're often shelved.

Everyone's an expert critic,
they judge your every word.
Some give naught to God or church,
but want their voices equally heard.
Your pour your heart to unhearing ears;
Gossiping women and distracted men.
The holy words of God you read,
not knowing if it reaches them.

You're compared to TV preachers,
though you're nothing of the sort.
I see you love your people,
thought you may get no support.
All you want is for your church
to serve your God and fellow man,
but getting some off of their ass
is more than most men can.

Never can your guard go down,
no carefree nights drinking with friends.
The actors, the athletes, the senators may have vices,
but one mistake would be your end.
Some may think you soft and frail
because you neither scream nor curse.
No one see the strength it takes
to be God's hand in world perverse.

Once I wished to preach the Word
in church from pulpit grand,
but I chose war instead of that.
Your stress is harder to withstand.
I've seen combat, I've seen death,
I've starved for days, I've been attacked,
but still I'd rather have that life
than know that weight upon your back.

So buck up there, preacher!
Let your smile be fast and real!
Eternal work is not in vain,
and some see how you feel.
Let your rest be in the fact
that God is working through your hands.
His will's not done in spite of you,
you're following His great commands!

WHAT BEAST IS THERE LIKE MAN

What beast is there like man?
What other being created so fierce,
so mighty,
so set on conquest?
What other creature mounts the frosted peaks,
where simple ascent burns lung and muscle?
What else can make arid wasteland its home
where life-bestowing water is little more than scarce?
Can others also thrive in rotted swamps,
sinister jungles,
bitter glaciers?
And after venturing all else,
to seek home and hazard
under seas and in the stars?
None other can do all, but keen
and ruthless man.

Does the truculent gull ponder the heavens,
or the severe lion the intricacies of sound?
Does the ponderous bison ponder meaning,
or the noble whale debate his place in the waters?
What else made by God creates philosophies
and meaning to justify existence,
or touches the clouds to speak across the earth?
Man does all, mastering waves,
virtuosos in music,
prodigious wordsmiths,
erectors of monuments,
flying higher than adroit eagles dare,
diving deeper than the monstrous ghouls of the oceans!

Then, finding none other his equal,
does man's aggression turns inward
in earth-shattering wars that threaten creation itself.
He fights himself to bring his paragons
to the zeniths of the earth,
raising potent fist to the awed sky,
which looks down in wonder and horror
at the Leviathans, champions, and chimeras in our souls.
What other but man
is so endowed by his Creator
with vigorous, warlike spirit,
finding savage joy in swinging sword,
thrusting spear, and silenced rifle?

What else but man is given
the weighty gift of love?
To grasp inamorata in softened embrace
with fell hands?
To feel devotion to sacred femininity
in fluctuating heartbeat?
To nestle blank tender childhood
to cherishing breast,
adoring, leading innocent progeny
across untraveled sands of experience?

WHERE THEY MEET

WHERE THEY MEET

There is beauty in conflict,
        the storm clouds that make
the sun's rays so lovely.

There is terror in love,
        of losing treasure unearthed
after toilsome searching.

There is wonder is war,
        in the lengths men go
to both live and to die.

There is fear in family,
        of ruinous actions
profaning divine gift.

There is power in battle,
        in using full lengths and breadths
that test limits of skill.

There is worry in life,
        returning to untrod paths
and uncertainty after survival.

There is a maelstrom of meaning
        in that frenzied plain
where they meet.

WARRIOR FAITH

Mikey the Mighty's a warrior for sure.
He grows a sweet beard, wears tactical pants,
posts picture with AR and pistol on hip.
But joining the mil? "I've got athsma, I can't."

"A Viking I am, of Norse blood so pure!
A warrior religion! To Odin I'll chant!"
He roars out with pride as he throws in a dip
while working eight hours at dad's power plant.

Achmed does not know about Mikey's Thor's hammer,
nor does he care how much Mikey can curl.
He lives in the sand with AK four-seven,
preparing grenades, to pull pin and hurl.

While one posts on Facebook (with terrible grammar)
about axes and heathens and Valkyrie girls,
the other will die just to get into heaven
for country and jihad and violence incurred.

"Ragheads are pussies!" yells Mikey the Brave
as he throws on his "Infidel" t-shirt so tight.
Though Vikings are gone and their legend has passed,
his war cry's, "Valhalla!" and, "Might Equals Right!"

Thought his arms are like sticks and his chest is concave,
Achmed is the one who will go out and fight.
Those Muslims, a warrior religion to last –
they'll fight us today, hell, they fought English knights!

He thinks he can fight, our posturing Mike.
He thinks he'll kill ISIS, Bushmaster in hand.
He'll do it while sipping a cold Viking ale,
firing one-handed from creaky deer stand.

One is my foe, and we're nothing alike.
I've fought him before on his own native land.
But versus a coward, he'd surely prevail,
against a fake Viking who thinks he so grand.

TRUANT BOY

Born, alas, too late
the dark young man before me,
to find desire abated
of blood-mad war party.

His grief upturned
at joining our beloved Corps,
this truant green boy
too late, too late to fight in our war.

The tales he'd heard
had turned his blood to fire,
but ended long war
had laid his hopes on a pyre.

He envies us our stories,
whether funny or darkness in depth,
for all he hears
is longform shibboleth.

"All that I wanted
was to take my place in the fight,
but the window is closed
for my courage to see the day's light."

"To be a heart breaker,
but there are no more hearts left to break!
To be a scalp taker,
but claimed are the trophies to take!

We try to say
that gratitude's what he should feel,
but words ring hollow
when we pity his plight so real.

How sad to be
a strong young man untested,
to never fight,
to win, or even to be bested.

MADLY

I ponder if doctors despair of the fact
that most of our ailments are caused by the lack of
good hygiene and diet and taking good care
of ourselves; of our bodies we're so unaware.
Does God see us just as those doctors so sadly?
His children destroy themselves living so madly.

DREAM

I dreamed of years
and narrow fears
in night's cold embrace
I called to my brothers
but I wore not their colors
nor carried their forsaken weight

INSOMNIA

In hours 'tween nightmares,
the bed is a robber of graves,
cradling aches in back and limbs
to mock them with echoes of pain.
Its gravity pulls rest from bones,
leaving residues of weakness
in sheets sticky with sweat
and weary with dreams.

NIGHT TERRORS

My wounded, lovely Valkyrie,
Magellan of my whiplashed soul,
bound by your eternal vow to me.
For you alone is the sight
of unmanned shape,
   your sorrowful skald.
You wear your covenant as steel,
a breastplate forged in pain,
   quenched in weeping.
Your helmet dented by
   iron-tipped words,
your greaves scarred by grief.
I roar your name in the shaking night,
my unconscious mind brandishing
   a cliff's edge of insanity,
yet your arms and heartbeat
remain a promise of forever.

DARK DREAMS

The Sleeper lay abed
during mournful drone of dawn's shrill wind –
    asleep at last in hands of night terrors.
Orgasmic rushes to the guns,
    hands trembling with ecstatic adrenaline
    as with a boy's first eager fumblings. . .
Let the dream curl its smokey tendrils,
    grasping the mind with vile, clawed hands . . .
The inward cries
    clotting into corpse-like fear
    as sights settle onto an atrophied soul, wrinkled from disuse
A dark dream, heavy and silent, sliding through the mind. . .
That darkness learned sorrows
    in the nights,
    studied them, absorbed them
    at ages most learned their first laugh.
Vanity swelled its flesh
    like a ripened corpse,
    bloated to bursting.
Hell nested in its heart,
    its vile brain rejecting the light.
Its lips were empty of the praises of God,
    its eyes unshaded by His glory.
Meeting it was a haunting
    of its plundering eye,
    and its words were curses
    falling from its mouth
    like black snow.
It loomed,
    dark of soul and terrifying.
That devil fought many a battle –
    The Sleeper fought its last.

PARCHED

The dryness is not even a promise of things to come,
a kiss of rain in advance of exotic embrace.
It is a void, a vacuum
pulling the very water from your living bones.
Parched thorns are withered hands of the dead,
reaching in frozen posture for monomolecular moisture.
Rocks crumble, mountains crack,
their stony tissues pulled apart under ultraviolet assault.
The dusts are the particles of the dead and dying,
casting off desiccated flesh in a violent shunting.
Yet here is man, scratching his survival upon baked land.
Even here he builds and plants
in a terraforming unique to the species.

LIONS

Imagining warrior traits during times of ease
  is remedied by exposure
  to black-fisted rogues, willing to die.
A man may be "Alpha" in the forced farce of peace;
  a lion in a zoo - patchy, pale of mane,
  in the midst of compressed souls packed in concrete.
Yes, he may flex and boast in his cage,
  roaring his theatrical wrath in colorful braggadocio
  to likewise caged gazelles
  until blood and nerve stagnate
  in modular mortification of the heart.
All of this may echo in dead chambers
  til he set foot back in the wild,
  where men and lions, dark-bearded and fierce
  rule the dust, jungle, and bones with jealous fervency,
  where the hunting is true, vital and vibrant,
      and scars are the currency of cheapened flesh.

TRANSITION OUT

What creates that missing bond,
that primaeval connection between men?
The covalent compound
of suffering and purpose,
the hydrogen and oxygen
creating thirst-quenching water
and mobilizing fire.
Thus matter fuses atoms
into new element;
brotherly love.

Naturally occurring in war,
an unspontaneous molecule
to be forged, laboratory-made
in peace and civilian life.

We seek what we've lost,
even without knowing.
Not provided or issued,
it must be sought out,
it must be fought for.

SOMETIMES NO

Our mamas, they each both prayed to our God
to watch o'er the dangerous paths we would trod.
Daily our wives both did ask of the Lord
for all of the grace that He could afford,
for Daniel and I, we both called Christ our friend,
but I would keep living, and his life would end.
A godly influence, a badass Marine,
Daniel was all that I wished I could be.
"If God watches over His Christians in war,
Daniel will surely be watched over more
than those who don't pray as a man really ought
to in combat and fear," was my general thought.
Then Fallujah decided to take him away
with double stacked mines one hot winter day.
He fell with nine others in belligerent blast
and turned a bright morn into bleak overcast.
Our prayers were the same, but that mighty man fell,
impugning my faith, a once proud citadel.
"God will protect us," I once thought so sure.
"My Lord is my rock and my heart it is pure!"
But I've since searched the Bible, my fear to disarm,
but God never said that He'd keep us from harm.
How foolish to ask of our Lord God for more
when we are the ones who beg for a war.
We can't control God, though maybe we try
to change course with prayer, there's a chance He'll reply;
No.

2031

In next raucous decade,
will we still be here?
Will ancient FOBs crumble,
fossilized, petrified
in a hungry, magnetic sand?

Near twenty years
we have trod here.
Time enough to end
one war, start another.

If we leave soon,
where will my son fight?

MY NAME IS VETERAN

A simple work was desired;
to hide and build in factory
       with honest, good hands,
denying inherent destructions with deceiving mind.

Efforts were made to be
       the man of gray,
camouflaged in normality,
but the clipped nature of direct voice,
the length of arrow-like stride,
hung a sharp-edged sign overhead
for all to read and know:

       "My name is Veteran"

Obvious and obtrusive were efforts to fit,
       like an ingrown hair festering
on a child's smooth face,
picked and prodded once discovered.

Rapid became requests of tales
       from life "over there,"
and answers gladly given.
In horror and shame the realization arrived
that it was I who held the damnable sign.

Pride in service was stepped beyond
and I trod in the realm of the starving, quivering,
       attention junkie,
tapping veins for the next ingratiating hit

Honorable would have been the course
that brought hard-won skill
and begotten strength to bear
in civilized use,

       but no.

Relished was the besotted title and whispering stares
that ended as two-edged weapon
       in failed assimilation.

SUICIDE

Allowing ink in soul to spread,
in time it fades, though
never to nothing.
Always it resides,
you always know
your blackened capabilities

COGNITIVE DISSONANCE

Deeply I believed
in the *truth* of inherent worth,
    that is,
until value was required of me
and performance necessary

HALF MAN
(THE LAMENT OF LCPL SHMUCKATELLI)

What do I do, Chaplain? What do I do?
I thought I loved her, loved her true,
but she took my heart and ran and ran,
Now I'm half a man . . . just half a man.

> Now I'm half a man, Chaps . . . just half a man.

I thought we started in such love and bliss,
Reveling each look and touch and kiss,
I thought loved she me ev'ry single day, but
now I see . . . She only loved me for my pay.

> Now I'm half a man, Chaps . . . just half a man.

I left to fight with gun and ruck and flack,
hoping she'd be there when I got back.
And she was true for days! Like or three or four,
Then she banged my neighbor like a common whore.

> Now I'm half a man, Chaps . . . just half a man.

Home I came to empty house and door ajar,
an empty bank account, a missing car.
She went to Vegas with her boyfriends, Chaps!
I barely got the working scraps.

> Now I'm half a man, Chaps . . . just half a man.

You tell me to love my wife,
but lawyers took away my life.
Now I live in barracks rooms all week,
while I pay her alimony . . . so she can cheat.

> Now I'm half a man, Chaps . . . just half a man.

She's never rucked for klicks or miles
with pack filled up with heavy trials,
but all the same, she still gets paid
fifty percent of all that I've made.

> Now I'm half a man, Chaps . . . just half a man.

I hear you cannot be a good Marine
or be a decent part of war machine
until you've lost at least one wife,
and given up to half your life.

    So now I'm half a man, Chaps . . . just half a man.

BLURRED FACES

A picture dangles in time and space
never displayed on friendly hearth
or prominent wall
Rather shoved in drawers
stored in drives
hidden from prying gaze

A tiny hand traces edge of paper

Dangerous men war tools in hand
stand feet planted in a conquering gaite
clothing and gear worn and filthy
a masticated smudge of tans greens and grays

Daddy who are they she asks
Voice high and pure as a bell
Why are they all dirty and icky

Theyve been through hell I want to say
Theyre my team and we had a dirty job
Is what I actually say

Is that you she asks pointing into the past
At a face that was grubby cocky smiling

Yes honey that was daddy
I dont tell her why we smiled
we had shwacked a bunch of dudes

Five five six
Seven six two
A10 hog from heaven

Daddy whats wrong with his face
She points to him on the far left

Countenance is hidden from lens
faces blurred with digital smear
faces blacked out with squares of night

Nothing honey its just blurry
Why
So one can know him

Names removed
an identitectomy

I cant explain to her
That guy is a SEAL now
This one is a Raider that ones SF
The rest contract guns for hire

All blurry faces doing cool guy shit
A great paradox in war
Do things so great that

No one will see your face
Know who you are
Read your book

Youre a Ranger a PJ
An 0311 who doesnt advertise
An eleven bravo without an ego

Why erase the face
Deny the name
Why take the picture at all

Leave only the mission and the team of
Pixelated ghosts

Glory eschewed
only the deed remains

TELL ALL MY GIRLS

How shall I tell all my girls of the darkness,
the terrible deeds that their father has done?
That fear that does lurk in their closets at night
was once their own daddy with ghillie and gun.

Their faces I touch with their love oh so clean,
lovingly holding the daughters I've known . . .
recalling the blood on my hands from the past,
crackling and black, though it wasn't my own.

the truth I hear,
the smell is fear, the violence all-surpassing,
their faces real,
their love I feel, affection yet amassing.

Their kisses and cuddles are the breath of my life,
that love undeserved on my finest of days.
My soul is a stone with callouses thick.
Such love is a gift for which I should pay.

"The bad guys" they see on their sweet tv shows
were pink little choir boys compared to my team.
We gleefully killed in the night and the day,
relishing death heard in every scream.

but they adore
their daddy more exuding love and kindness...
should I deny
that little lie, continuing their blindness?

I teach them to love and be kind
and to pray to our God for His guidance in life,
yet *I* recall turning my back on our Lord
while hoping and fighting to enter the strife.

My arms that were holding them tight to my chest
have carried a gun and have held dying men.
These lips that have kissed them and spoken words sweet
have asked for revenge for the death of a friend.

I've cried the tears
across the years, and hated with a passion,
but oh so sweet!
to call defeat! to a daughter's own compassion!

They look at my uniform bright (oh so bright)
and think I was *placed* 'tween the evil and them.
They do not know that I *asked* to be sent
to bring chaos and hell in Iraq and the 'Stan.

They'll ask me one day of my job in the war,
and whether or not I have "killed men for real."
What do I tell all my girls on that day?
Do I bolster or ruin their image ideal?

there is no blame,
I'm not ashamed of blood I've spilt for brothers,
but daughters three,
just leave me be . . . now go and ask your mother.

ABSENCE

one hopes in the fondness brought
to the heart by the sweet ache of absence
but the healing heart of mankind turns it
to a boulder in a yard
easily circumnavigated

The longer the absence
the more frequent the trips
the more deeply trod is the path around
until its removal is a shock

PRAYERS

I have prayed to my God
(indeed, my life is but a series of prayers),
and defined my world by His providence.
Drawn out, exuberant thoughts of great length,
and bow-shots spit at the sky in rapid fire.

Daily I beseech for my wife and children.
It never ends (and never will) in the love
I share with God for them.

I have prayed for safety in times unknown.
In my youth I've asked for it,
though old age, experience, have lessened such desires.

Strength I have requested, for myself and my men
(a natural boon for war-men in dire need).

I have begged for laughing vengeance
for brothers wounded and dead,
dear friends "mangled to morsels."

Requests for godliness, righteousness and purity
have mingled with cries for forgiveness,
issued deep from blackened marrow.

In prayers of my heart,
my death-song played too near to be melodious.
Yet deeper still in the pit I lay,
forgotten by love, disgraced by fear;
on the day I began to pray for the man
who would love my wife,
raise my children,
build my home
after I die in this God-stricken land.

FALLUJAH MAN

I saw you first in the
bland sand of the tan streets,
Fallujah man.
I tucked my rifle tighter
in my spider hole for
       watching,
                waiting
for events to transpire.

Your body slumped with
unseen weight
      wait
           Is it fate
           for you to be my kill on this date?
I slowed the racing rate
of my heart and breath as you
turned corner into straightened road.

You carried no weapon,
      no bomb,
           no device to do me harm
in your thin, brown arms.

No, it was your world you carried . . .
      a small baby boy.

How I envied you, Fallujah Man,
as scene did drift through scope.
Releasing pressure from trigger,
I dared myself to hope
to one day have as much as you,
oh lucky, blessed Fallujah Man,
to carry my world in my arms,
a father's delightful plan.

DEAD RECKONING COLLECTIVE is a veteran owned and operated publishing company. Our mission encourages literacy as a component of a positive lifestyle. Although DRC only publishes the written work of military veterans, the intention of closing the divide between civilians and veterans is held in the highest regard. By sharing these stories it is our hope that we can help to clarify how veterans should be viewed by the public and how veterans should view themselves.

Visit us at:

deadreckoningco.com

@deadreckoningcollective

@deadreckoningco

@DRCpublishing

Follow Cokie

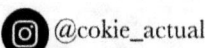 @cokie_actual

COKIE is a vituperative redneck who spent his formative years in a seminary, then performed the obvious transition to military service. After doing bang bang things for pew pew people, he picked up a pen and discovered that it was significantly more convenient than the sword (at least regarding his wardrobe). Despite (or perhaps because of) multiple blows to the head, Cokie continues to use the Oxford comma. He lives in the midwest with his beautiful wife and children where he contemplates service to God and the absurdity of braille road signs.

www.ingramcontent.com/pod-product-compliance
Lightning Source LLC
Chambersburg PA
CBHW062115080426
42734CB00012B/2876